STREET MUSIC

CITY POEMS

by Arnold Adoff

illustrated by Karen Barbour

HarperCollins*Publishers*

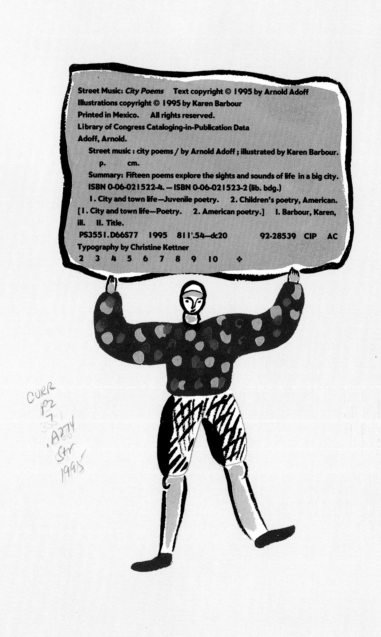

Street Music: *City Poems*   Text copyright © 1995 by Arnold Adoff
Illustrations copyright © 1995 by Karen Barbour
Printed in Mexico.   All rights reserved.
Library of Congress Cataloging-in-Publication Data
Adoff, Arnold.
     Street music : city poems / by Arnold Adoff ; illustrated by Karen Barbour.
          p.   cm.
     Summary: Fifteen poems explore the sights and sounds of life in a big city.
     ISBN 0-06-021522-4. — ISBN 0-06-021523-2 (lib. bdg.)
     1. City and town life—Juvenile poetry.   2. Children's poetry, American.
[1. City and town life—Poetry.   2. American poetry.]   I. Barbour, Karen,
ill.   II. Title.
     PS3551.D66S77   1995   811'.54—dc20   92-28539   CIP   AC
Typography by Christine Kettner
2   3   4   5   6   7   8   9   10   ❖

For Jaime Levi and Leigh Hamilton
— A.A.

To Nick,
my best buddy
— K.B.

Open Window

The clock on my dresser
shows almost six but the
garbage truck is the alarm
as they empty cans along
our street and fling black
sacks of garbage into the
back of the open truck.

It is easy
to say
c l a n g
  b a n g.
It is easy
to hear
c r a s h
s m a s h.

The clock on my dresser
shows almost six but the
garbage truck is my alarm
this too early morning.
I can just see the first
sun shine on the back of
the truck as it moves
                    down
                        the

                    street.

There is A Wading Pool in Our Park,

a swimming pool for the bigger kids,
and a bathtub full of cool water
later on when I get back home.

But right now the h y d r a n t
is open and t h i s s t r e a m
of water gu sh es out in an arc
of
ice
wet
fun
so cold we shiver in the steaming
                                                    summer
                                                              sun.

There are rainbows
through the highest
splashes of water,
through the highest
reaches of water,
through the highest
curves   of   spray.

Cold wet colors this hot day.

The Streets Are So Hot:

sidewalks, cement sidewalks
bubble under our rubber
soles
as we walk.
The
swee
wee
sweeper truck
sprays water
do wn the
gutters
and
raises a fine wet mist up
to
our knees.

Steam
rises.
Sidewalks, cement sidewalks
stretch flat and c o o l
again under our fe et.
We
w a lk
ho me.

From This Bus Window

From this bus
                   pulling away from the curb
I can stretch
m y n e c k. I can just stare i n t o
                     the eyes

of a b i c y c l e
m e s s e n g e r :
h e   i s   t h e
         meat
o f
t h e
   s a n d w i c h
     b e t w e e n
      this bus and the moving van
          on his other side.

Then he blows the whistle glued between his lips,
and s p r i n t - p e d a l s o u t o f t h e s a n d w i c h
and s l i d e s ahead of us both: bus and van,
and a r o u n d
his cor ner.   We ride on.

i Was Born Here In This City

but I still look up at   the
                        m a g i c
of tall buildings
pushing through the clouds.

   One dry autumn afternoon
I lay down on the cool sidewalk in front of the down-
town office tower. And all
the people   had to walk
around me, because
I wouldn't stand
up until I had
seen the
clouds
move
over
the top
of that stone
giant, or the top
of that giant building
move   through   the clouds.

I was born here in this city
but I still look up at   the
                        m a g i c
of tall buildings
pushing through the clouds.

On The Way To Breakfast Sunday

On the way to breakfast
Sunday with cousins, we
walk through this down-
            town
               park.
A man plays guitar
while a woman sings and
a single dancer glides
               alone
around   the   fountain.

Boys on skateboards, girls on in-line skates.
Joggers in shorts, joggers in sweats. An old
woman walks with a cane. An older man within
his aluminum walker nods down to my face.
Early morning mothers with carriages rock
                        and
                       watch.

Pigeons with   red eyes
peck at empty c r a c k
               v i a l s
in short
     grass   under   trees.

Ants And Grass Hoppers,

spiders and centipedes,
and all assorted crawling creatures
who work and play and go to school:
crowd the streets each afternoon
as they climb up sub way stairs
and follow sweet crumb trails
to bank corner cash machines
for green leaves that pay rent,
and dry cleaners,
and book stores.

They buy sugar,
        buy flies.

This Woman With Two Daughters

spends her days in the cold shade
of the bank cash machine doorway.
Mom gives her a dollar: stuffs it

into the empty coffee cup she has
in her s t r e t c h i n g hand.
Every afternoon the same: walking

through avenue crowds we always
see them seated on their c a r d-
b o a r d, sharing   cut   fruit.

We smile.   They stay.   We go.

Music Moves Us Along The Street

The music is in the street block by block moving us along.
In front of the corner restaurant this guy is playing his cello
and growling out a song about a girl. A man has pulled an old
upright piano onto the sidewalk and chained it to the chain link
                                    fence in front of the vacant lot.
He plays with fists and elbows
while his feet do a sandpaper
shuffle to the beat. The old fiddler is sitting at his usual place
                    telling stories of his early times in this city.
                    Four young players with speaker amps and an
                    electric generator are blasting their heavy
                    rock louder than the roar of the subway trains
                                        under   our   feet.
                                        We snap   fingers.
                                        We   snap fingers.
                                        We   snap
                                                    fingers.

Music moves us along the street.

Street Music

This city:
the
always
 noise
 grinding
up   from   the
s u b w a y s
u n d e r
 g r o u n d :
slamming from bus tires
and taxi horns and engines
of cars and trucks in all
v o c a b u l a r i e s
                                        of
clash
flash
screeching
hot metal l a n g u a g e
 c o m b i n a t i o n s :

as   planes
overhead
roar
an
orchestra
of rolling drums
and battle blasts
assaulting
my ears
with
the
always
noise   of
this   city:

street   music.

Always Engines

Day
and
or
night
this city
is not
really burning
only
seems:
as
sirens
are the
songs of
day
and
or
night
in
this
city.

Stay away
from our
b l o c k.

This Coldest Winter Weekend

Morning: we can bundle into coats   and scarves   and woolen
gloves inside leather gloves   and   fast walk
down the streets and through the park   to the
a l w a y s   o p e n   carousel.

The flashing horses are turning around   and my
still-cold hands still hold their reins.   The music
and my horse   rock me   up and down   for this winter
ride to n o w h e r e .

Then hot chocolate before the bus ride home.

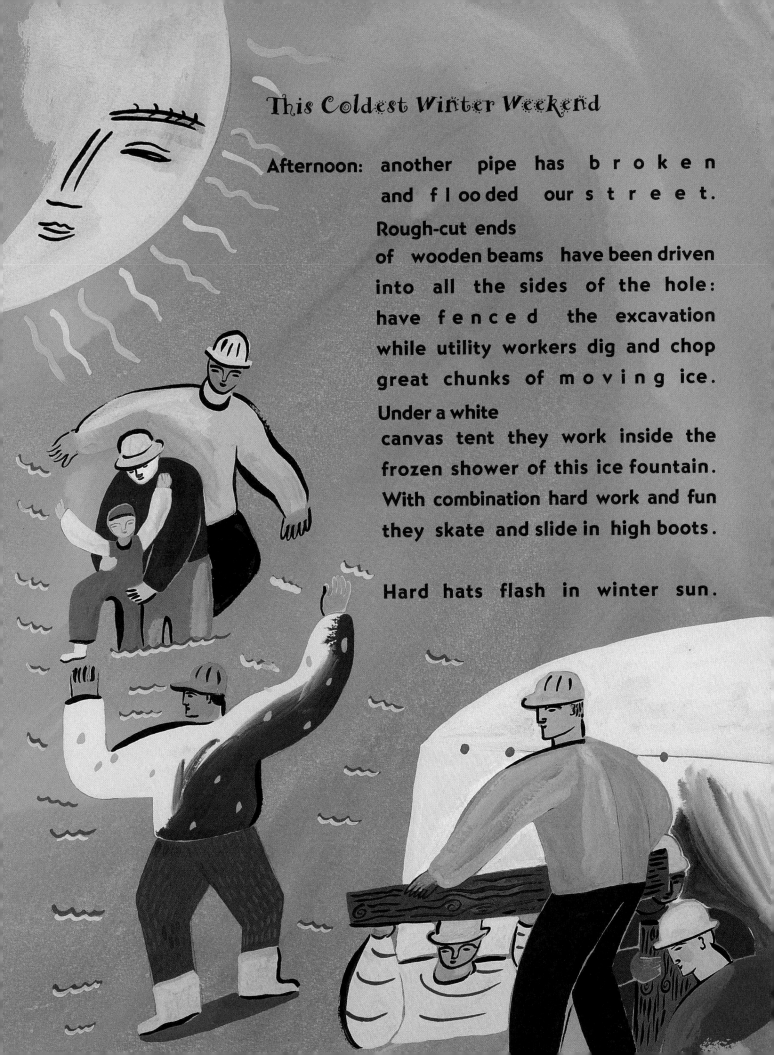

This Coldest Winter Weekend

Afternoon: another pipe has b r o k e n
and f l oo ded our s t r e e t.
Rough-cut ends
of wooden beams have been driven
into all the sides of the hole:
have f e n c e d the excavation
while utility workers dig and chop
great chunks of m o v i n g ice.
Under a white
canvas tent they work inside the
frozen shower of this ice fountain.
With combination hard work and fun
they skate and slide in high boots.

Hard hats flash in winter sun.

On Our Avenue Of The World

First
warm
evening of the world: people fill all the sidewalk space between open shops and parked cars. We slow walk through crowds of languages and clouds of steam from carts of c o o k i n g foods.

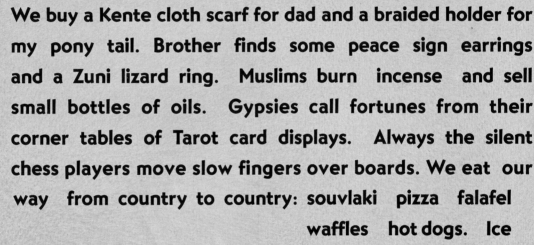

We buy a Kente cloth scarf for dad and a braided holder for my pony tail. Brother finds some peace sign earrings and a Zuni lizard ring. Muslims burn incense and sell small bottles of oils. Gypsies call fortunes from their corner tables of Tarot card displays. Always the silent chess players move slow fingers over boards. We eat our way from country to country: souvlaki pizza falafel waffles hot dogs. Ice
cream
and
ices:
colors of faces
on this
avenue of our world.

Late At Night

after I've been sleeping, I wake up because the covers are on the floor. The apartment is dark and quiet. Only the numbers on my dresser clock shine through. I pull open the curtain of the window by my bed, and look out and across my street,

and down the avenue. There are always people on these streets. This avenue of never-ending lights is some bright river between dark buildings, under blackest sky. Cars move all night, through greens and changing reds. People move through the doors of the famous pizza place. Spotlights shine on piles of fruits and vegetables in front of all-night markets. Women and men come out of the subway on their way home, and stop to buy fresh oranges. Women and men buy containers of coffee and muffins at the corner bakery,

then go down into the subway, on their way to work. A police car races down the avenue, sirens screaming. An ambulance follows close behind. The people who sleep in doorways, or on the subway grates in the middle of the avenue, are bundled into blankets and boxes for the rest of the night.

I close my curtain until morning light.

Arnold Adoff is the noted author of over thirty books for children and young adults. BIRDS, BLACK IS BROWN IS TAN, and FRIEND DOG are a few of his many picture books. His books for middle-grade readers include SPORTS PAGES, a Reading Rainbow featured selection; a biography of Malcolm X; and THE POETRY OF BLACK AMERICA, which he edited. In 1988 Mr. Adoff was honored with the NCTE Award for Poetry for Children. He lives in Yellow Springs, Ohio, and New York City.

Karen Barbour's paintings have been shown at galleries around the country. A commercial artist as well as a children's-book author and illustrator, she has written and illustrated the acclaimed LITTLE NINO'S PIZZERIA, which was a Parents' Choice Honor Book as well as a Reading Rainbow featured selection, and has also illustrated Arnold Adoff's FLAMBOYAN. Ms. Barbour lives in Point Reyes Station, California.